Responsibility

Julie Murray

abdopublishing.com

Published by Abdo Kids, a division of ABDO, PO Box 398166, Minneapolis, Minnesota 55439.
Copyright © 2018 by Abdo Consulting Group, Inc. International copyrights reserved in all countries.
No part of this book may be reproduced in any form without written permission from the publisher.

Printed in the United States of America, North Mankato, Minnesota.

052017

092017

 THIS BOOK CONTAINS
RECYCLED MATERIALS

Photo Credits: iStock, Shutterstock

Production Contributors: Teddy Borth, Jennie Forsberg, Grace Hansen

Design Contributors: Christina Doffing, Candice Keimig, Dorothy Toth

Publisher's Cataloging in Publication Data

Names: Murray, Julie, 1969-, author.

Title: Responsibility / by Julie Murray.

Description: Minneapolis, Minnesota : Abdo Kids, 2018 | Series: Character
    education | Includes bibliographical references and index.

Identifiers: LCCN 2016962331 | ISBN 9781532100123 (lib. bdg.) |
    ISBN 9781532100819 (ebook) | ISBN 9781532101366 (Read-to-me ebook)

Subjects: LCSH: Responsibility--Juvenile literature. | Responsibility in children--
    Juvenile literature. | Children--Conduct of life--Juvenile literature. | Social
    skills in children--Juvenile literature.

Classification: DDC 179/.9--dc23

LC record available at http://lccn.loc.gov/2016962331

Table of Contents

Responsibility

Responsibility is all around.

Do you see it?

Sui helps at home.

She **scrubs** the dishes.

Sam makes a list of **chores**.

He is responsible.

Jim takes care of himself.

He brushes his teeth.

Aly tries her best! She gets good grades.

Oops! Pat spilled his water.

He cleans it up.

Ian is on time for class.

His teacher is happy!

Dora walks her dog.

She is responsible.

Were you responsible today?

Some Ways to Be Responsible

Clean Up After Yourself

Do Your Homework

Take Care of a Pet

Take Care of Yourself

Glossary

chore
a common task around the house or yard.

scrub
to clean by rubbing hard.

Index

abdokids.com

Use this code to log on to abdokids.com and access crafts, games, videos, and more!

Abdo Kids Code:
CRK0123